THE NEXUS INITIATIVE

the neXus initiative
Brent Henley

Written with Jeremy Broussard
Edited by Jennifer Ritter
Author photo by Gwen Aucoin

ISBN 978-0-578-48840-0

This is a short book about
the business of giving.

Foreword

The word *networking* isn't working anymore. At its core, the word was meant to imply connecting with others. However, "networking" events have become increasingly difficult places to make a true connection. Tell someone you would like to meet their network and they'll likely withdraw. Those who are interested in networking are really just out to get something from you. Somehow, in the past several decades, our understanding of "networking" has evolved into something less than it was originally defined.

At the same time, if you're responsible for growing an organization's bottom line — sales, leadership, customer service — you still need to connect with others.

So do I.

That's when I started looking for another way. Left empty at a networking event, I found that we needed another, better, more genuine way to grow business. So I began listing what was noticeably absent from modern networking:

1. **No one's listening.** That was easy to see. The rooms are full of people who want to talk to you, but no one really wants to listen to what you have to say.

2. **No one's solving anything.** When it comes down to it, we need solutions —

solutions to balance our budget, solutions to reduce cost, solutions to stop the printer from jamming. In a room full of people who simply want you to hear their pitch, it's difficult to solve any real problems.

3. **No one's providing value.** The ultimate way to grow business is to provide value. At networking events, most people are rushing around trying to get value…from you. In a room full of takers, no one's giving.

What if we could build a new system of interacting with each other that solved these issues?

What if we did something fundamentally different and opposite to typical networking activities?

What if we turned networking on its head, shifting it from a "taking" activity to a "giving" activity?

And that was the beginning of *the neXus initiative*.

x

It's not networking

"What is it these individuals really want?"
"They want clients," he said.
"Then give them clients."

The (first) neXus.

One of my clients called to ask about networking. He wanted to grow his business, but he wanted to gain referrals in a way that wasn't contrived or cheap. He was asking me for answers I'd been pursuing for years.

What if there was a way of "networking" that wasn't really networking at all? What if we could change the system from a "let's see what I can get" to "let's see what I can give?" What if there was a higher level of business thinking that focused on helping everyone around us succeed?

Would that work?

In over 20 years of consulting, leadership training and strategic business development, I still couldn't find a single, true professional who felt completely comfortable at a "networking" event. The ones who claimed to love networking were often the people my clients worked to avoid — overtly sales-y, insincere, cheesy, hollow — the descriptions may sound cruel, but you know the type.

In that span of years I developed a new theory — the best networking wasn't even "networking" at all, at least not in the modern sense of the word. I started to believe that there would come a day when our business interactions would evolve from a "take" to a "give" activity...and it would work even better than before.

What I was considering wasn't new. It had been tested and proven ages ago by a guy named Ben Franklin (yeah, *that* Ben Franklin). Somehow the method got lost in the digital age.

Somewhere in the 80s and 90s we felt like the way we approached people needed to change. The world was going digital and our attitudes and expressions needed to match the fast pace style of that era. We told ourselves that quick pitches and fast hand-shakes were important to a generation that seemed to value rapid, shallow interactions. Between Franklin and fiber optics, we replaced relationships with techniques.

Now, a client was asking *is there another way?*

In a point-and-click-instant-gratification world, is there a way to grow business beyond the "see what I can get" system we call networking?

Yes, I said.

And we were going to prove it.

Is he crazy?

This particular client worked in the financial services sector in Salt Lake City. His desire was to approach particular individuals to discuss the possibility of working with him. He called me for advice, saying he wanted a productive approach, but one that was also sincere and honest.

I told him something I'd learned years ago: One of the best ways to sustain or build a relationship with someone you already know is to give him a valuable, meaningful gift that helps him solve a problem. To know what to give him, though, you have to know what he needs and wants.

That's where we opened the dialog:

"What is it these individuals *really* want?"

"They want clients," he said.

"Then give them clients."

I imagined his face while listening to the silence. I could almost hear the questions in his mind.

How are we going to give new clients to potential customers?

How on earth is that going to help me?

The gift of neXus.

I explained how a neXus works. I told him
the difference between neXus and
networking. I described how sharing this
simple idea then providing potential clients
the opportunity to create a neXus of their
own might very well be the best gift he
could give...and valuable gifts are one of
the best ways to build and sustain
relationships.

So he gave the gift of a neXus — in the
form of an event. It began with a simple,
personal invitation that went something
like this:

"I'd like to give you a gift: Meeting people
you've never met to help increase your
sales. This is an invitation only event from
5:30 – 7:00. The gift is called neXus and
it's an activity unlike anything you've seen
before — you will leave with five to ten
potential new customers."

In his phone and email discussions he was
sure to describe that this wasn't some
ribbon-cutting or mixer and there would be
no gimmicks. And though they would meet
a lot of new people, this was not a
"networking" event in the modern sense of
the word.

Curiosity alone may have fueled
attendance, but the promise of leaving
with five to ten new clients hardly went

unnoticed. Before we knew it, my client had 200 RSVPs for our first neXus event.

Typically atypical.

The event looked ordinary, in many ways, right down to the hotel conference room (after all, there are only so many places you can host an event for 200 people). My client, always a gracious host, provided complimentary food and drinks. At first glance, guests must have thought this event was an "After-Hours" networking social. They were in for a surprise.

While the guests ate, we made a short presentation about what a neXus was, about how networking, in the modern sense is broken, about how it's time to create a genuine approach to promoting our business…and tonight we were going to practice one way of doing just that.

We discussed the difference between giving and taking. We explained that many modern networking events prompt us to take. In other words, we hand out our business card and talk about ourselves.

This event, however, would be different. To participate in the neXus initiative, everyone in the room would be required to give. That's right. The people in the room were going to solely look for ways to give something to the people they meet. This could be helpful advice. This might be a client referral. This could be a connection to someone else they just met. This might be a promise to follow up later with a solution. How participants gave was left up to their own creativity. What was important was that they met people with giving (not taking) in mind.

Giving, I said, required three things:

1. Listening

2. Solving

3. Providing Value

If they couldn't accomplish these things, they were to politely tell the person that they enjoyed meeting them and make a graceful exit.

Success is in the cards.

To make it measurable, each participant was instructed to *receive* five business cards. That's right, they were to ask for cards, not hand one out (unless asked). Then, while listening, they were to figure out the answers to a few questions:

- What are this person's challenges?

- What are this person's successes?

- What are this person's short-term goals?

They were to match what they heard with resources they might provide. If they could help, they would do so then or promise to follow up.

Let's get giving.
In the beginning, I could hear a bit of uncomfortable laughter. After all, this was new territory for most professionals. It was as if no one had instructed them to give before.

But that changed quickly. By the time we reached the thirty-minute mark (our allotted time for the exercise), it was almost impossible to get everyone back to their seats. It seemed that nobody wanted to stop *giving*.

When asked for feedback, the responses went something like:

"I got to know more people in a better way than any networking event I've ever been to."

"Several people heard about my service from other people in the room. Because I was helping them, they were inclined to tell people about me."

"I ended up with more referrals in 30 minutes than I've received in the past month."

It turned out that, as participants met each other, they identified other people in the room (many of whom they'd just met) who might help with problems, successes or goals. Listening to one person opened up opportunities for others and they were glad to *give* the connection. There also wasn't a need to "pitch" or "sell" their business because many of the other 200 people were doing it for them, in a genuine, problem-solving way.

They asked for more time. They were having fun, helping people and building their business connections at the same time. At their request (and with permission from the hotel), they kept giving until for well over two hours past the event's scheduled conclusion.

So you see, even in the modern digital age, *giving* is valuable, after all.

The beginning of a positive epidemic.

I couldn't have told you this at the time, but that night wasn't the end of the neXus initiative. I still receive feedback from participants, letting me know that their neXus has helped them grow in ways they'd never imagined. My pioneering client continues to use the method and continually gets connected with genuine, interested clients as a result. In fact, he continues to connect with referrals from the neXus.

We planted a seed.

Like all seeds, they grow slowly at first. Every now and then, someone in another market would hear about the initiative and inquire about starting her own. I'd help in any way I could. Sometimes that meant putting on another workshop. Sometimes that simply meant talking with her by phone. Whatever the method, it seemed everyone who contacted me liked the idea of changing business growth from a "taking" activity to a "giving" activity.

For many of them, a mixed approach was the best way to start. "Keep your sales force on track," I'd advise. "Keep your goals. Keep your methods. Just add the neXus initiative to what you're already doing." After all, I added, "Your sales people can almost always afford to have lunch with someone once a week. That's all it takes to incorporate the neXus initiative to your existing sales system."

The neXus Initiative

In the pages that follow, we'll reveal the mechanics of a successful neXus. It can be free (depending on where you meet), you don't have to pay dues and I don't know anyone who's tried this initiative and not enjoyed themselves.

You'll also find:

- It's not "relationship selling" or networking in the modern sense of the word.

- It's based loosely on an old, proven principle of mutual cooperation, updated for our tech world.

- It's surprisingly simple and surprisingly effective (the best things always are).

- For the equivalent of one lunch per week, you can start giving (and receiving) solutions and advice with real value.

This is the work of a group intent on changing the way we do business. They're not takers and they never want to be. They're givers, and because they associate with other givers, they have all that they need to grow continuously.

Participating in this initiative means joining this positive epidemic. It's a small but growing number of likeminded professionals eager to grow their own businesses...by helping you to grow yours.

Why "Relationship Selling" is broken

"When I walked into my bank today, I saw all kinds of signs about how important my relationship is with them...but I didn't recognize anyone there and, frankly, they don't recognize me."

What's missing?

As is the case so many times, I learn as much from my clients as they learn from me. They're the ones who first said to me that "networking" or "relationship selling" is broken. They're the ones who prompted me to start thinking of how to promote business in a new way.

I remember looking intently at a group of small business owners gathered for a focus group. They were there to talk about relationships — business relationships.

What was missing?

What was it that some organizations did right?

What was it that so many seemed to do completely wrong?

That's when one of the participants stood up and said something I'll never forget, "When I went into my bank today, I saw all kinds of signs about how important my relationship is with them."

The crowd seemed to nod. They knew the signs he described. Smiling faces. Shaking hands. The words "Trust" and "Friends" in large print.

Then he added, "But I don't recognize anyone there and, frankly, they don't recognize me."

Another business owner backed him up, "I can't find companies that truly build relationships and it is hard to find sales people with those skills...*relationship selling* is broken."

What relationship?

There was a big push in the 90s for everyone to move to "relationship selling." Everyone needed to get closer to their customers. Following this, a series of tools flooded the market. The new tools (mostly database-type contact managers) helped us keep notes about clients so we could remember not only their phone numbers but their likes, dislikes, hobbies, favorite pet, hairstyle, sister's name and more.

For about 20 years companies built their brands around these "relationships" with customers. Over the past decade, sales enterprises have increasingly embraced relationship selling as a way to "transform their transactional forces to increase referrals" or "align with their brands and increase sales in hyper-competitive environments" (at least that's the industry jargon).

While we made these "relationship investments" Internet businesses matured. The new online operations made sales transactions simple and quick. Virtual relationships don't require face-to-face interactions. The online purchase process taught customers that having a relationship with sales people simply wasn't required... nor was it important.

So the moment we reached the dawn of "Relationship Selling" we began to enter an age when it would never solve the problem. Or, I should say, it didn't solve *any* problem.

And that's what was always broken.

Knowing your client's shoe size and favorite sports team doesn't make you a resource. It doesn't give you value in their eyes. It doesn't build trust. (Neither do glossy signs with smiling faces.)

This is what matters: If you really want to have a relationship with clients, help them.

Don't try to impress them by demonstrating that you remember their child's middle name (creepy). Help them in the most meaningful way possible. Figure out their challenges. Find real solutions. Show them you're thinking about their goals. That's problem solving. That's providing value. That's what was always missing from "relationship" selling.

The old game.
Does this sound familiar?

"The other day my company sent me to a 'How to Get More Referrals' seminar. So I put the techniques to use and got lots of referrals from my friends and associates. Problem is, the referrals were worthless and my friends don't speak to me anymore."

We've trained each other to believe that business relationships are somehow different than every other relationship.

We've confused ourselves into believing that friends are supposed to simply "give us business" in the form of their personal database, sacrificing the privacy of their friends, family and colleagues for the sake of our professional growth. If there ever was a recipe for killing relationships, that's it.

To add insult to injury, we bought into the concept that, if our friends and associates don't do this for us, there must be something wrong with our *technique*.

Do we ever hear a spouse say, "I married him/her because they have such good relationship-building *technique*?"

Do we ask our associates, "I'm looking for someone to be my friend, can you send me a few referrals?"

Do we apologetically request, "You know, when I wanted to spend time with you, I used poor technique. I've learned some new techniques, though, mind if I try them out on you?"

Techniques never built a relationship. Value does. Our spouses, friends, trusted colleagues and best customers count on us because we have value to them. We enrich their lives, their work, their business and more. And there's only one way to become valuable...to give.

There is no game.

Why are business relationships so difficult to forge? They're not. It just seems that way if you're using the old game.

The truth? There is no game.

Sure, relationships can be skewed. We use each other, trick each other, scheme and distort what people think is true. We do this in small, seemingly insignificant ways like white lies and broken promises. We do this in large, detrimental ways like unfulfilled contracts and bait-and-switch tactics. That's game playing. (Not only is it a game, it's a short game.)

No matter what, it's better in the long run if those techniques are never considered relationship building. Some of us get away with it for a while. Some of us even "get rich quick" on the notion. But in no way is it beneficial to all involved. So, while *techniques* may build databases, leads, sales reports or other things, they don't build relationships.

Plus, in a world that's more connected than ever before, getting away with these techniques is more difficult than ever before. This is why we're finding the techniques are failing us. As the world becomes more educated, connected and communicative, consumer intelligence continues to grow quickly and the old game slowly dies.

But one method of building relationships remains. It has outlasted all others. You can witness it at small tables in a local diner. You can witness it at negotiating tables for heads of state. In fact, it's present any time two people want to build a long-term relationship.

That method is …

The Law of Human Reciprocity

In every relationship we've ever built, we've always encountered the Law of Human Reciprocity. It goes something like this:

> *I get what I give.*

It's that simple. In fact, if you learn nothing else from this book and only take away that maxim, you have gotten your money's worth.

Remove this principle from any relationship and it will begin to deteriorate. Marriages. Partnerships. Congregations. Friendships. And yes, business associates. Without this fundamental maxim, no long-term relationship ever sustained itself.

Let's look back at our decades of sales and referral training. What about those *techniques* in this context? The same principle applies. Any training experience that does not include this maxim cannot be considered relationship building. It might "get you in the door" or "bypass the gatekeeper," but it will not build relationships because relationships, in any form, are built on giving.

Why?

Because giving is the only thing that creates value in a relationship. Giving is the currency for how we value one another.

In fact, a positive relationship, as it pertains to people, should be defined as a state of reciprocal giving. If one person ever stops giving, the relationship suffers. Stop for too long and it completely dies.

Failing Systems

The reason most sales/training/referral systems fail is that they often demand that you *receive* value before you *give* value.

Sometimes they require you to get a referral before you ever give one.

Sometimes they want you to get a sale AND get a referral immediately following each sale (they want you to GET twice, without even giving a thing).

I call these people *takers*. With all this taking, there's simply no room for a relationship to form. That's because no one in a dynamic like this is giving anything of real value. Eventually, it fizzles out.

Imagine a friend who only comes around when he needs something from you. How long before you start avoiding that person? How long does it take for you to realize that what you are experiencing is not a relationship?

My guess: Not long.

I don't have to know you very well to perceive that you know a good relationship when you see one. That's because — business, friend or otherwise — good relationships are enjoyable experiences.

Yet we keep teaching each other in sales schools, orientations and throughout the business culture that we should receive without giving. Then we wonder why our employees aren't building relationships. We question lack of customer retention. We wonder why sales numbers decline.

These are all common symptoms of a failing system. As far as failed "relationship-building" systems go, there are examples everywhere. Here are my three least favorites:

Failed System #1: Asking people (especially clients) for referrals is a dumb proposition.

I bought insurance once and after the policy closed, the guy asked if I could give him five referrals. I looked him in the eye and said "No."

(That's when he looked at me like I had three heads.)

Perplexed, he fumbled for words. Obviously his *extensive* sales training had not prepared him for this particular response. Somewhere in the mumbling and paper shuffling he managed to ask me why I wouldn't give him any referrals.

(Of course, I was prepared for this question.)

"Because you haven't given any to me," I said bluntly.

I allowed some time for him to consider this "new" concept, then added, "Look, I just bought a policy from you, don't you think it's appropriate for you to reciprocate in some way?"

He still had that puppy-listening-to-noise expression (you know, the cocked head and crossed eyes). So I explained, "You meet people all the time who might be able to use my services and you haven't asked them to connect with me. You haven't sent me one referral, yet I still purchased this policy from you. Now you're asking for...of all things...a referral from *me*?"

I wasn't upset, but I definitely want the people I work with and buy from to understand the Law of Reciprocity. In this instance, the concept was not only foreign, it had literally been trained *out* of this person's way of doing business.

(It did make for entertaining conversation, though. I suggest you try it if you get a chance.)

We began to discuss the entire referral process. That's when he started to come clean about his sales training. He admitted that when he asked clients for referrals, they feel cornered. They feel obligated to at least give up a few names...and that's exactly what they're doing. They're throwing out a few sacrificial offerings to keep the sales gods from demanding more.

He was *taught* this. He was literally taught to ask for referrals this way (sometimes I still have to repeat that to myself because I find it so difficult to believe that we train people to put their friends, family and associates on the spot like this).

So we talked about how this makes his new customers feel. The process goes like this:

1. A potential client takes the time to listen to his pitch.

2. She considers the options.

3. She asks any clarifying questions.

4. She (hopefully) buys a policy.

   (Now the unexpected happens.)

5. She's asked to sacrifice five of her friend's and associate's contact information.

He worked to build her trust. He took the time to explain his service. He invested energy to build a positive buying experience. In the end, he leaves her feeling what?

Run over.

Is it smart to do all that work building trust only to abuse it the moment they've signed a contract?

Hardly.

She feels like she just gave him business and he wants more. Now, she just wants him to go away. In the worst case scenario, he gets put on her "people to avoid" list and she stops talking to him altogether.

And those leads she gave, he can't count on them. She was NOT giving names of people who really need a product or service. She gave the names of people who would get least upset if a salesperson called them unexpectedly.

This system has failed so often that we see it coming from a mile away. I've received apologetic phone calls from friends who regret mentioning my name to a salesperson after being cornered for a referral. "I'm sorry," my friend said to my voicemail, "I just didn't know who else wouldn't mind getting this call." Or, "You don't have to buy anything. I just told him you might listen to what he's got to say."

It's a shame that corporations promote brand statements about relationships only to train their people to ruin them immediately following a sale.

It's a shame that this type of training is so ubiquitous that we almost expect it.

It's a shame that some salespeople are taught that this failed system is the only way to succeed.

There is another way...and it's more consistent, more respected and has made more successes than any technique or cornering question.

Failed System #2: Networking (in the modern sense of the word) is dying.

We all know it when attempts at networking are going poorly. It's painfully easy to spot.

- It's in the cheesy smile of an overbearing salesperson.

- It's in the coercive look of a friend who suddenly "needs your business."

- It's in a million clammy handshakes, zippy one-liners and trade show winks.

These are signs of *takers*, people who want something from you. They're easy to notice and, if you're like most, you've sharpened your skills at avoiding these people.

Before the days of takers, networking didn't always have such a bad rap. Originally, networking was a shiny new term for meeting new people. The expression began innocently enough, but there's no changing its modern definition: *Taking*.

Walk into any event labeled networking and you'll likely find a few takers (or more). They're walking around looking for ways to get prospects, get leads, get referrals, get business…whatever the name, it's centered around "what you can give to me" or, in sharper terms, "what can I take from you." All too often, everyone in the room is so focused on taking, there's no way to receive anything of value.

That's how, no matter how nice some of these events appear to be, the activity can become remarkably unproductive. That's also how we can find ourselves at a networking event with hundreds of people and not leave with a single thing of value.

The room was full of takers.

There are millions of ways to meet people. There are millions of places to find givers. Beyond that, there are millions of people who would love to give us the things we're looking for, whether that's a lead, prospect, referral, client or just plain old help. If you're living in the networking model, you may find this difficult to believe, but *networking* (in the modern sense of the word) is no longer our best option.

Failed System #3: Working alone is impossible.

We live in a world that's increasingly populated by small businesses. It's becoming more common (and easier) for almost anyone to be an entrepreneur and that's made this world an exciting, interesting place to work.

When I compare successful and unsuccessful businesses, both past and present, one trend is clear: No one goes it alone.

So many startups have the value to give. They have the expertise. They have the work ethic. They seem to have it all going for them. But what they don't have is a circle of trusted advisors. They don't have a group of people to give to. Consequently, they don't have a group of people giving back to them.

Every business success I've ever witnessed happened with the help of a group. Every business leader I've ever known rose to the top with the help of a group. Proven leaders surround themselves with a circle of helpful, trusted advisors who not only give them ideas and referrals, they give them constructive criticism and warnings.

No one goes it alone.

The original marketing

"In the autumn of the preceding year, [1727] I had form'd most of my ingenious acquaintance into a club of mutual improvement, which we called the Junto." — *Benjamin Franklin*

"No-marketing" marketing.

There was a time when professional organizations such as the American Medical Association and the bar association frowned upon advertising in the way we think of it now. They felt that each professional practice must be built on integrity and service, not marketing hype. So doctors, financial advisers, attorneys, bankers and others simply "hung a shingle" outside their offices and opened for business.

Or at least it seemed that way.

In today's world of 24-hour news and 60-second infomercials, we look back in disbelief that there was a time when marketing seemed *optional* for professionals.

How did any business survive without marketing?

It may surprise you, but the key to their success centered around many of the principles we just discussed. What may surprise you more is that the practice is alive and well today. In fact, many professionals, sometimes even entire organizations, find success with this timeless method before they ever spend a dime on modern marketing. Some don't have a marketing budget at all.

He called it the Junto.

Benjamin Franklin didn't invent the technique, but he certainly added his wisdom to the process. Franklin, who owned a printing press, organized a group of professionals in his hometown into a club of sorts. The group, called Junto, was comprised of several non-competitive business leaders. Before they joined, they agreed to promote the mutual success of other members. Franklin credits the group for much of his early business growth.[1]

This concept flourished in America. It wasn't long before professional organizations sprouted up in every community and, in a world without Internet connectivity and mass media, joining one of these groups was the best way to let others know about your new business.

This is the unseen, second-step of professionals who appeared to simply "hang a shingle." They joined local groups and service leagues. They became part of organizations like Rotary, Chamber of Commerce, Lions Club, Kiwanis and more. In the process of public service, they made friends, learned about the community and, over time, obtained that prized possession...that business gold standard... the referral.

---

[1] Many Juntos are still around, most notably the London and New York Juntos organized around the financial sector.

The cart and the horse.

I'm not advising you to slash your marketing budget. I'm not telling you to start a new business without advertising. I'm not saying you'll never need a well-designed logo or a functional website. I am saying that, way too often, we put our (marketing) cart before our (relationship) horse.

The real workhorse, the real way to haul our brand out to others who haven't seen it is through people. It starts with the people you know. It grows by giving.

The best companies.

I'm often asked about word-of-mouth marketing. How does it work? Why is it that the best companies just get business by word of mouth? How can we do that?

Is it because they have some great logo or home page?

No, that probably came later.

Is it because they launched a nationwide marketing campaign?

No, odds are that came later, too.

No matter what business you're in, no matter how much (or little) you spend on advertising, we know that nothing sparks growth more effectively than referrals. So how do certain companies always seem to magically get them?

Every successful brand succeeds around a core momentum of referrals. In fact, I'll wager that you probably gave a referral today. Here's how:

- A friend mentions she's thinking of booking a flight. What favorite airline comes to mind? Which ones do you advise against?

- A colleague is looking to buy a new car. What brand do you recommend? What brand do you warn about?

- A visitor is looking for quick, delicious food while staying in your home town. What place is best? Which place should be avoided?

From food to flights, we give referrals for top brands and bad brands every day. Odds are, we receive referrals as well.

For winning brands, this is the holy grail of marketing. They know that nothing gets people investing in their product or service like a genuine referral. They also know that referrals might occur from an advertising campaign, but mostly, they come from genuine relationships. We know now that relationship building is not networking. It's a neXus.

The neXus initiative

"I often hear people say that growing a business requires cold calling. Boloney. I hear that growing a business requires advertising. Bull. I hear that growing a business requires a web page for $9.99. Think again. The greatest businesses — the ones where the brand speaks for itself and customers tell others about them — operate on the principles of a neXus."

What is a neXus?

A neXus is an environment where your business grows out of integrity and your brand speaks for itself. In other words, no gimmicks, no techniques. People know what you stand for and they tell others about it. Not only that, their opinion travels far and wide, reaching new people every day.

Then you do the same for them.

Imagine a group of people eager to let others know about their favorite brand — and that brand is *you* (or your product or service).

What would happen?

Potential clients would call you out of the blue. They will have already heard good stories about you. They call simply because you provide exactly what they need and they would like to meet with you as soon as possible.

That's *not* networking.

That's neXus *working*...for you and them.

It's working because you have taken the time to build a fabric of mutually beneficial relationships. How did you build it? By giving.

That's a neXus. Building one is simple, but there are some concepts and steps that work better than others. For example, it helps to know three basic rules. To put it bluntly, once we launched the neXus initiative, we found three things that absolutely kill a neXus. It's important to know those rules before you start.

The First Rule of neXus: Know your brand.

If I haven't consciously thought about my brand (why I exist, what I want to accomplish) then it's difficult for anyone to promote me. They can't describe me because they don't know how. And when no one can describe you, no one can recommend you.

Note:

Brand is not an elevator pitch. Don't get me wrong, it's good to have an elevator pitch. It's just better to have a good brand.

Brand is not your slogan. A lot of people confuse brand with slogan. Slogans change repeatedly. Brands endure.

Brand is not your logo.

Brand is not your advertising.

Brand is not your brochure.

The design of all of those things come after you've formed your brand.

Brand is about one thing: **Values**

There are three or four values your organization (or you personally) will ultimately stand for in the market. They are the values that you will adhere to under pressure and cling to in the face of obstacles.

These values become the filter through which you make your decisions about who your customers are, who you hire, how you go to market and more.

Your brand is what you cling to.
Early in my consulting career I struggled with accepting certain offers that didn't match my brand. These were cash offers that came at a time when my budget was lean, to say the least. What they wanted me to do was simple: "put butts in seats" (so to speak). In other words, train as many people as quickly as possible in order to "maximize the training contract." That's corporate consultant speak for "make more money without necessarily providing value."

I had very different ideas about what training should look like. I felt that simply filling a room and sling-shotting information to a group might be a way to make money, but it wasn't what was best for the client (or students) in the long run.

I had to make a decision.

Do I take the job because I need the money? After all, I was new to the business. I needed the work.

I declined.

Eventually (it took some time), people heard about me and the values I stood for. Some of them hired me. I made it through the slump.

In the end, I found that "eating" was a temporary problem. Changing my brand, however, was permanent. If I took a job that didn't fit my brand (my values), I'd forever be known as "that guy" who will do anything for money. It would be difficult to build my reputation after that.

So I tightened up my budget and kept my brand intact. That's when I learned what a real brand was about. It's something you hang on to, especially in tough times.

Your brand is your story.
I liken the word brand to a story. After all, that's what you're writing. When you live your brand, you write a story for yourself. You also write that story for other people. To know your story, simply ask two questions:

1. What do people think of when they hear my name (or company name)?

2. What stories come to mind?

Brands create a set of stories, mental images, concepts and ideas that come to mind when we simply hear a name. I'll prove it.

Imagine your least favorite relative. (Everybody's got one.) When you hear his name, what stories come to mind?

From your perspective, that's his brand. That's the experience you have of that person all wrapped up in a neat mental story. That brand-story may be different from others in your family. Everyone has an individual experience. But those stories were created in your mind by someone who consistently did or said certain things in a certain way. Those things formed a collective story ... a brand.

What story does your brand tell?

What story does your company brand tell?

This is how the world will think of you.

To trust or not to trust.
Think of the brands you don't trust. Why don't you buy their products or services? What are your stories about those brands?

Un-trusted brands are used out of necessity, if at all. Trusted brands are not only used, they're recommended. Over time, there have been some brands in my life that I've always trusted and recommended. For example:

Campbell's Soup — I've got a hundred memories or more about a simple can of soup that often costs less than a dollar to purchase. The brand is so consistent that the stories in my mind have never changed.

Zapp's Potato Chips — Louisiana's local chips are crispy and bursting with Cajun-Creole flavor I can't find anywhere else. When Zapp's are an option, I know I'm going to enjoy the snack.

Apple — No tech company has provided me with products in a more intuitive, reliable, easy-to-enjoy way than Apple. They were the first products I bought that didn't need a manual or require hours of learning time. For me, that's valuable. I simply haven't found a better user experience with any other line of tech products.

Nissan — Everybody has their favorite car. For me, it's my Nissan Murano. The story it tells me is one of comfort, performance and reliability. I like it so much I'm considering buying another one.

Disney — Whether I'm renting a movie or taking a vacation, I always know I'll have a consistently entertaining experience. The story this brand tells me is about smiling faces, quality experiences and fun.

Rouse's Market — I never thought a grocery store would make this list, but my locally-owned Rouse's has built something more than a grocery store. I go there to explore new cheese, wine, nuts, soaps and more. Their obvious attention to detail tells me I'm buying quality food, the local selection makes me proud to shop there and the variety turns grocery shopping into a small adventure.

Hardy's Cleaners — Hardy's is my locally-owned dry cleaning service. One day I knew I wouldn't make it to the store by closing time, so I called and asked if he could stay open so I could pick up my clothes before flying out of town. He said, "No, but if you tell me where you live, I can drop it at your house." I still tell this story to everyone who needs a good dry cleaner.

What are the brands you trust?

Why?

Your brand is a promise.
A brand is a promise to do what you say.

Saying one thing + Doing that thing = Building your brand.

Say one thing, do another...not good.

Why am I going on so much about brand?

Because the strength of your neXus cannot exceed the strength of your brand.

If you create this neXus and don't keep your promise, then you give permission to others in the neXus not to keep their promise. (Then, you don't really have a neXus, you just have a loose group of affiliates.)

Brand Exercise

Because knowing your brand is so important to a productive neXus, I suggest working through this short exercise before you get started.

Think of three words that answer this question:

What three words come to mind when others hear the name of my company (or, when they hear my name)?

1._____

2._____

3._____

Now for the test. Find five of your closest friends and ask them the same question. Jot those words here:

_____

_____

_____

_____

_____

_____

Compare the list. Are you projecting the image you think you're projecting?

The Second Rule of neXus: Your role in the neXus is not to promote you. (It's to help your neXus.)

The next two rules are short and easy to remember. It starts with knowing your role, which is to *give*.

This is a core concept that's critical to the whole system. You are not in a neXus to serve yourself (taking). You are there to find opportunities to genuinely give to others in your group.

When you meet, you're there to find out about them. You're there to listen to what's happening in their world.

What do you do with that information? You promote them.

We're told as kids that sometimes we need to toot our own horn, but is it ever as effective as when someone toots it for us? Never. So one of the best things you can do to energize and support your group is to promote them every chance you can.

I have found that this state of mind — promoting the members in your group — is so important, I consider it vital to the group's existence.

The Third Rule of neXus: Be a giver (not a taker).

I tried to contact Mother Theresa several years back and realized she didn't have a phone number. She didn't have a fax line. She didn't even have an email address.

Can you imagine operating a business without a phone number? Can you imagine operating an organization without an email address? Most of us put these things in place before we even have our legal documents in order.

How then, did Mother Theresa run an organization that made possibly the greatest global impact in our lifetime when she didn't have any way of communicating with the outside world?

She *gave*.

She gave so effectively that others carried her message for her. She gave so honestly that others trusted her. She gave so authentically that she built a brand, a story that the whole world knew.

No advertising. No gimmicks. Just giving.

Did she go without food or money in this process? No, people heard of her brand and supported her efforts with donations. Did she lose staffing? No, people heard of her work and joined her mission. Did she succeed by taking? No, she gave until she died.

In for-profit and non-profit ventures, funding comes from different sources, but giving works the same. If we gave to our clients the way Mother Theresa gave to hers — honestly and earnestly — we would always have more business than we could handle.

Giving is the first step of any relationship. It's also the key to continuing any relationship.

So give…and don't look back.

Build your neXus.

The neXus Initiative, in its simplest description, is a small group of business people who promote each other. It's that straightforward.

We have found that certain factors make some groups work better than others. For example, structured activities help keep groups together (Franklin incorporated this concept to keep the Junto together). Simple rules (the three you just read) can help you avoid having your connections fall apart. Practicing certain principles can make your group even more productive.

But putting a basic neXus group together is pretty easy. It takes five steps to set up a neXus. When you spot opportunities for improvement in a manner that fits your style or business, by all means, grow with it.

First: Find eight people who would mutually benefit from the neXus initiative.

I initially thought 12 people would be the magic number for an active neXus group. As it turned out for most participants, eight was more manageable. This allowed them to actively help members of the group while still maintaining their own client needs. So, while there's no required number of people, you'll see in Step 2 why eight members (not including you) works well in the beginning.

Choosing the right eight people.
Someone in the cubicle next you is not the best choice for your neXus. Why? Because we found that the healthiest groups are made up of a diverse cross section of people, careers and interests. Odds are, the guy in the cubicle you have lunch with every day is a lot like you. These people are great friends, but they might not be able to expand your reach as well as someone more diverse.

A good fit: I have a client in New York who knows a great tailor. Tailors know people who need good suits. People who need good suits need services from my client. This makes the tailor a great fit (pardon the pun) for his neXus.

So how do you come up with a diverse neXus? Start by thinking of the services and goods your clients often need.

- Do they need legal advice? (Find an attorney for your neXus.)

- Do they need capital to grow? (Bankers, venture capitalists, financial advisers and others might make a good fit.)

- Do they need help with recruiting? (Recruiters, HR professionals, workforce officials and more would fit this need.)

- Are they facing employee challenges? (Consider HR professionals, CEOs, Chamber of Commerce leaders, counselors.)

- Do they often interact with government officials? (Think of people you know who serve in government, inspection services, government contractors and more.)

Being able to connect your clients to good, reliable solutions will become the cornerstone of your neXus. So start by asking what your clients really need. The answers to those questions point to the people who will work best within your neXus. That's because they might be able to help your clients and your clients might be able to help them.

To get started, ask yourself: *What are five of my clients' most common business needs?*

1. _____

2. _____

3. _____

4. _____

5. _____

Next, ask yourself: *What are five of my clients' most common personal needs?*

1. _____

2. _____

3. _____

4. _____

5. _____

Who do you know that can help them with these 10 items? Those people are a great fit for your neXus.

Once you've developed a list of diverse participants, jot down their names and keep it handy.

Here's the chart I use in workshops. Unlike a standard networking diagram, connections between everyone in the group must be symbiotic. That interaction is symbolized by reciprocal arrows.[2]

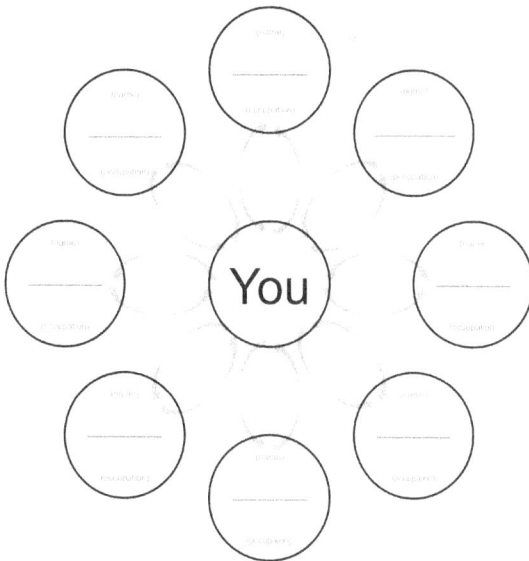

My neXus group.

To give you an idea of how my group works, I've included a copy of my neXus below. Of course, I've changed the names, but these are their actual professions.

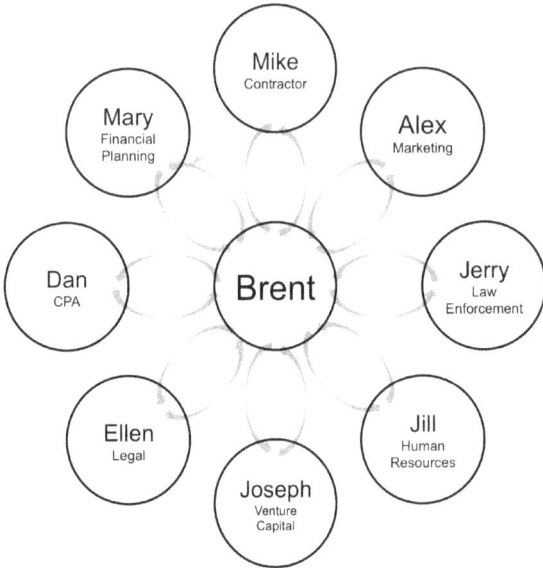

I'm a consultant, yet almost everyone in my neXus is from a field unrelated to consulting — or so you might think.

After working with my group for a while, something interesting occurred: The general contractor connected me to more referrals than anyone else in the group.

How did that happen?

Since he specializes in remodeling, he's often hired by successful career professionals. As he gets to know them, he asks about their business. Quite often they mention struggles or challenges that fit within an area where I might be helpful. Because he's in my neXus, he mentions me as a resource. He contacts me with a request to see if I can help his client. I do what I can...and that sometimes means they become a new client for me in the process.

These happy accidents are perhaps the most amazing part of the neXus process. Traditional sales and networking programs could never have connected me with these clients because they ruled out the potential of an unrelated connection who simply wants to help me...because I help him.

Second: Explain the neXus Initiative.

The next step is pretty obvious, but it's worth thinking through. Here's where you tell each those eight people that you'd like to help each other grow each other's business through this thing called the neXus initiative. Explain it in your own words (Or explain it in complex terms, quote the book if you like. However you go about it, make it genuine.)

What's most important is that you explain the two core commitments required to be part of the group. They must commit to:

1. One meeting (lunch, coffee, etc.) every two months

2. Help each other when the opportunity arrises

You can talk about the rules, you can talk about the principles, but the simplest way to explain this concept is with those two commitments.

Use your judgment to determine her interest. If she seems hesitant, don't get pushy. (The last thing you want is to make someone feel pressured.) If she seems eager to try it out, check her name on your list and tell her you'll call for a meeting in the coming weeks.

Third: The once-a-week meeting.

As I mentioned before, I originally thought 12 people would make an ideal neXus Initiative. We have a natural tendency to think, "The more people I have in my network, the more business I'll get."

But this is about giving, not getting — and you only have so much time to give. After all, you'll need to be serving your clients, too.

So after several test cases, we found that the greatest number of people most of us can effectively serve through a neXus is eight. Here's why:

Most of us, no matter how busy we are, can find time for lunch, coffee, drinks or some other casual meeting at least once per week. Meeting with one person in your group each week means you'll have met with everyone in the space of two months. This meeting cycle is not only manageable, it's just the right amount of time to catch up on what's changed since you last met.

The three questions.
At this meeting, your goal is to find out all you can about what's changing, what's working and what's not working for one member of your neXus. In today's busy world, this is the perfect mix of keeping your neXus member top of mind while staying abreast of your weekly career needs. Specifically, ask each other about three things:

1. Recent business challenges

2. Recent business successes

3. Goals for the next two months

When you know each other's challenges, you can begin thinking of ways to help. Perhaps more importantly, you've made a mental note about that challenge. Wherever you are in the coming weeks, if you run into a similar situation, you may find yourself in a position to help them once more.

Knowing their successes allows you to praise your friends effectively. Remember, "tooting your own horn" never comes across well, but someone else can praise you all day long. When you praise people in your neXus to others, you're giving them one of the best possible gifts.

Lastly, knowing their goals makes another mental note, an opportunity for you to help in larger ways. If she says, "My goal is to meet an expert who specializes in this particular field" you may instantly think of someone who could help. If not, you've got two months to encounter just the person she's looking to know. Knowing her goals puts you in position to help in perhaps the most positive, business-building way imaginable.

A note about the three questions.
You'll notice that I didn't ask you to bring your latest brochure or mention your elevator speech at this meeting. Those are networking techniques. While they might be catchy, they don't work effectively in

an authentic, mutually beneficial relationship.

So drop the sales speak. Can the brochures. These meetings are about how you can help your neXus friend. It's a brainstorm session and, for approximately one hour, you're her best consultant, advisor and supporter rolled into one.

Fourth: Grow by giving.

Here's the fun part. You've assembled your group. You've met and listened to what they need most. Now you get to be their greatest ally.

Your existing colleagues.

The first (and obvious) part of this step is to connect your neXus with people you already know. This is the quickest way for them to feel the immediate, positive effects of joining your neXus Initiative.

As always, make it genuine. The connections you receive from your neXus can only be as valuable as the connections you give.

Your new colleagues.

The second (and perhaps not-so-obvious) part of this step is to connect your neXus with people you have yet to meet. Yep — strangers.

If 75 percent of your future business comes from people you've yet to meet, the same is true for your neXus group. This means that meeting new people not only provides a way for you to grow, but you've now increased the odds of having a productive conversation by introducing them to someone in your neXus.

You'll also find that talking about your group to others changes the nature of conversations in a very genuine way. Every time you meet someone new, there are eight people who could potentially benefit from knowing that person. You're in a position to compliment your group. You're in a position to solve problems for your group or the person you meet. The neXus initiative not only provides you with a never-ending source of genuine conversation, it can position you to be a resource to more people than ever before.

Exercise: Receive five business cards at each event.
When you're at an event, it can be difficult to know how successful it was from a business perspective. That's why we gave the first neXus attendees a goal: Receive five business cards.

When focused on receiving cards, we mentally switch gears from talking to listening. Our mode changes from taking to giving, especially in ways that might help our neXus.

So change how you measure events. Start measuring success by giving.

1. First, use a clear and measurable goal — receive five cards. Pretty simple.

2. Second, focus on helping your group with each person you meet. In this mindset, the odds of being able to help increases dramatically.

Lastly, remember that there are eight people out there doing the same thing for you. (I can't think of a better reason to smile.)

Fifth: Maintain.

After two months, you'll have met with each person in your neXus...and all you'll do is talk about how you can help each other grow.

You're exchanging resources.

You're swapping advice.

You're sharing experiences.

Perhaps most importantly, you're making those mental notes about each other that will position you to help throughout the next two months — whether that's a referral, assistance with their goal or an opportunity to help them with a particular challenge.

Providing value — helping — is the sustain phase. Remember, providing value is how relationships sustain themselves. When you're helping your neXus, you're sustaining that group relationship.

When interest wanes.
What about when one person seems to lose interest? What if one person doesn't make their commitments? That's when maintenance is needed.

When you think someone's lost energy, give them one last shot with an offer of tangible assistance. Send them a referral. Connect them to a problem-solver. Give one more way, one more time. Then, if it doesn't work, find another person to take his spot in your neXus.

There's nothing lost. You've helped someone.

By and large, most people want to help others. Sometimes, though, we end up in relationships where we're putting all the energy into it. Your neXus Initiative is supposed to be a mutually beneficial relationship, which has to be symbiotic.

The best group works together for the good of everyone involved. That's an essential part of the system.

Givers in a takers world.
Know upfront that there are plenty of people out there who cannot understand Franklin's principle of giving as a way of growing business. Franklin knew this, that's why his group was small and made up of only the people who understood the value of mutual assistance. Takers weren't welcome.

Our job in this neXus movement isn't to single out the takers, it's to find the givers. It's a changing world, one that's filled with an ever-growing number of people who understand what Franklin knew as a higher level of success — mutual success. Building a successful neXus means finding those people. And they're everywhere.

All together, now.
Begin with your brand — that's your driver. Your brand literally drives you to wake up and go to work each day. Start by identifying that story so you can explain it easily to others.

Then assemble a neXus group. This is the mechanism you need to move from where you are to where you want to be (by

helping them reach their goals). Meet one
member of your group each week.

You will get what you give. That's why,
lastly, you'll need to continually fuel the
group's growth by meeting strangers.

Here's a map of what that looks like,
including a few principles we'll discuss in
the next section:

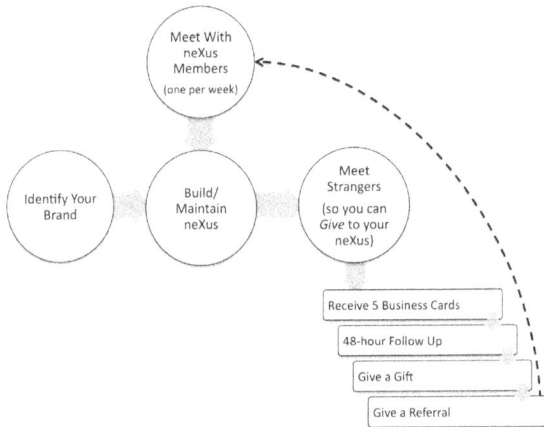

Principles of a neXus.

"Tis the business of little minds to shrink; but he whose heart is firm, and whose conscience approves his conduct, will pursue his principles unto death." — Thomas Paine

Know the rules, live the principles.

When we put the first neXus initiative together, it became clear what the rules of the neXus would be. Everything has rules in some basic way.

What I call rules can be thought of as prerequisite understandings. You have to know them *before* you can begin. Not doing so would be like trying to lead a football team without knowing how many yards it takes to make a first down.

Once we know the rules, though, it's *principles* that make us successful. I'm a football fan, so let's continue our football analogy:

- Players who know the rules can play the game of football. This has nothing to do with their skill, but rather it's the minimum standard to play.

- Better players know certain *principles* of the game. For example, they know that daily practice will help them improve during game time.

- The best players follow, practice, hone and adapt the *principles* on a daily basis. These are the pro players.

To put it simply, principles make us better. When followed to various degrees, principles separate regular teams from good teams and good teams from great teams. They are a part of every systematic life process and the neXus initiative is no exception.

As with all systems, certain principles do not become obvious until you've learned the rules and started playing. Others seem to appear right away. In practicing the neXus initiative, certain principles became immediately evident. Others appeared over time. Plenty came from others who shared their experience with me. Here are my most-used favorites.

The Stranger Principle

What does almost every business sales training program have in common? The division of our population into four main social types — quadrants. This is no accident. When we study human behavior, four distinct personalities almost always emerge.

These four styles also have one thing in common: They tell us that about half of the entire population will tend to initiate a social interaction, while half won't feel comfortable initiating that same interaction.

Other ways of saying that:

- Half are shy, half are not

- Half are introverted, half are extroverted
- Half are external, half are internal

However you slice it, if the world is truly divided into four quadrants (and there's plenty of research to support that), then only 50 percent of people in this world are going to approach you. The other half, by definition, is waiting for you to initiate contact.

That means, unless you're willing to cut your potential in half, you're going to have to meet some strangers. It also means that meeting strangers is one of the best ways to build a neXus and support a neXus at the same time.

Know how to meet strangers.
It's a world of abundance, you just don't know it yet. Or rather, you just don't know THEM yet. Remember our rule of thumb: "75 percent of your business will come from people you have yet to meet." Meeting strangers is the fuel for any neXus. Here's how to turn up the heat.

You can take the traditional route and head to business after hours and ribbon cuttings and other business events. Clubs offer a great way to meet other people. Almost every community has a Kiwanis and a Rotary Club.

But here's where people get stuck: the same people show up at Rotary, business after hours and ribbon cuttings. The reason these groups aren't always beneficial in the long term is because there often aren't any new people there. No strangers. That means the 75 percent of people you haven't met are at some other event.

So what's missing?
What's missing is a venue where you can meet new people in a business setting. That means you'll have to reach beyond the local clubs. These are my favorite three places to find strangers in a business mindset:

- **CVB** — I like the convention and visitors bureau website. If there's a convention in town, it's bound to be full of strangers in a business state of mind. I go to that hotel for lunch. View their exhibit hall. Perhaps most importantly, when I bump into someone there I simply *ask questions*. (More on this later.)
- **Business Journals** — Business magazines, journals and email newsletters will list upcoming business meetings. These are great places to meet strangers. The meetings are often open to the public. Show up with some genuine interest in what that organization does for the community and you'll likely find lots of people with enthusiasm and an eagerness to talk with you.

- **Trade Shows** – Don't get tied to your booth. In fact, I've had more beneficial interactions at trade shows when I walk around the place rather than sit in a booth. Ask questions. If you find a match, let them know you have a colleague who might need their services and get a card.

Does it feel awkward?

People who know the benefit of meeting strangers almost always have a more productive neXus. However, when we go to familiar events, the natural tendency is to find our group of friends. Humans want to be comfortable...but growth never happened within a comfort zone:

- I've never met anybody who rode a bike the first time he tried.

- The first time I threw a football, it felt awful, weird.

- We all feel uncomfortable when we open a new software program.

- Anytime I get into a rental car, the first five minutes I feel pretty uncomfortable. How do I turn on the radio? The wipers?

If you're feeling like this when you're meeting strangers, you're doing it right.

A word on meeting strangers.
Remember, meeting strangers does not mean networking. You're aim is not to take but to give to the people you meet and to your neXus.

The question principle.
I ask people in my neXus workshops to become insatiably curious about others. We humans love to talk about ourselves. It's a great equalizer and establishes commonality.

In a "take" system, we're taught to give our elevator speech, practice our pitch and make sure the person we just met leaves knowing the finer points of our company.

In a "give" system, these techniques bomb completely. Givers value time and attention. They value listening. They value genuine feedback. There's one way givers do this consistently: Ask good questions.

Givers understand how to sustain a genuine conversation with good questions. They start broad:

"Have you been to one of these before?"

"What do you know about our speaker today?"

After a few questions, you'll know if it's okay to get personal. One of my favorites: "Where were you born and raised?"

I meet so many people all over the world who don't work in the town they now live in. The resulting conversations are often rich and interesting no matter what their answers may be. Interestingly, I've often asked this question to one of two colleagues, only to find the friend turns and says, "I didn't know that! I always thought you were from here."

It's amazing to me how seldom we ask genuine questions to one another. There's so much to learn. People are fascinating and the stories are endless.

Talk about work afterward.
There's one, surefire way to come across as heavy handed and sales-y, and that's to ask a stranger about work before you know her on a very basic, personal level.

You don't have to understand someone's life history before talking about work. But understanding something as simple as why you're both standing in the same place means a lot to most people. It establishes your respect for her as a person. Then, and only then, is it appropriate to ask about other possibilities, particularly those relating to work or career.

The follow-up principle.

If you wait longer than 48 hours to follow up with anyone, you've greatly reduced the chance that person will remember who you are.

And remember, your job isn't to follow up in order to help yourself. Your job is to follow up in order to help someone in your neXus.

The genuine referral principle.

When you're actively promoting your group, you'll find yourself making more referrals. Part of the essence of a good neXus is a good referral.

When I meet someone I want to refer to my neXus, I start by telling him, "There's someone I know who may be able to help you (or may benefit from your help)." I might explain what a neXus is so he understand that this is a trusted reference. Then I tell him:

"I'll have him call you."

This is important because the person you're talking to has a reason to begin trusting you — but he doesn't know the person you're referring just yet. It's your responsibility (to all parties) to make a sound and reliable connection.

Call your neXus member and say, "Mike, I met this guy who's got this issue. I think you might be able to give him some advice." Not, "Here's a potential client for you Mike, go make the sale." Again, no taking. Even Mike needs to give.

It's critical that neXus referrals move forward with the same question in mind: "How can I give, serve or help this person?"

Connecting people to those you know and trust is fun and easy. It's one of the primary ways to energize a neXus group and it's like sending your clients a trusted expert every time they have a need.

The give-first principle.

We've heard it a thousand times growing up:

You get what you give.

That's the backbone of this process. But many of us don't realize that it's best to give *first*.

You see, introducing someone to your neXus concept and making them a part of your group is how we set up the framework Franklin knew was essential to organizational success. Giving them help *first* is how we provide value to the relationship.

Relationships with no value end up with no participants. Those with value rarely have an empty seat. This is true for companies, households and anything in between.

Giving first has a few added benefits. It shows you're genuine. It shows you're committed. It shows them that you're sincere about growing business through giving.

Besides, inducting someone into your group only to sit around and wait for her to help you is just another form of taking.

Give first. See what happens.

The open-minded principle.

Once you write off the possibility of anyone being helpful to you, you've written off building a worthwhile neXus.

Everybody has a network of friends. That means you might be pleasantly surprised that a tailor can be just as helpful to you as a corporate vice president (sometimes more so). I've found that those who open their mind to asking genuine questions and give their time to *anyone* truly experience the most active, productive neXus.

The solution-gift principle.

After you've given your time asking questions, the next best gift is one that provides a solution to the person you met.

That's why we've found that the best gifts in a neXus environment are gifts of information. For example, as I read business magazines, certain articles trigger recent conversations. So I go online and send links to the article or the white paper. Sometimes I'll even clip the article and put it in the mail. This does two things:

1. It lets them know I was truly listening. I can't think of anything more flattering or a better proof of character than showing someone that you're truly listening to them.

2. We're all busy. No one has time to read every industry article. If I can save them some time and link them directly to something that speaks to a pressing issue, I've truly given something helpful.

Here's a real-world example: Samuel Culbert, a business professor at UCLA, researches that most dreaded annual activity, the performance review.[3] Culbert's research shows that performance

---

[3] If you'd like to order it, here's the full title and info: "Get Rid of the Performance Review!: How Companies Can Stop Intimidating, Start Managing—and Focus on What Really Matters" by Samuel Culbert. If you're subject to performance reviews, I highly recommend this work.

reviews aren't helpful to employees or employers. In fact, they're most often a waste of time.

(I couldn't agree more.)

So when I heard about his book, I immediately thought of several clients, neXus members and potential clients who have struggled with this issue for years. This was just the kind of expert information that would be helpful to them. So I ordered a few copies and notified those people that the book was on its way.

All of them thanked me. A handful requested appointments to discuss this further. This is the kind of gift that makes you a resource. Nothing, I repeat, *nothing* will make you more successful than being a valued resource.

The listen-first principle.

My wife wanted a new vehicle and I decided to tag along during the purchase. We showed up at the dealership and the salesperson immediately focused on me. He described the vehicle to me. He laid out its benefits to me. He handed me the keys for a test drive.

After about 20 minutes, I surprised him when I said that I wasn't there to buy a car…my wife was.

Here was a person so focused on selling, he overlooked the person who was there to buy. Listening would have sorted this out, but when we have a "take" mentality it's easy to forget to give time and listen.

Take-techniques revolve around talking. But since talking doesn't necessarily solve any problems, it can leave customers feeling under-appreciated in the end.

Giving techniques revolve around listening. Because you took the time to listen you are uniquely qualified to be a resource. If you listen first, on principle, you'll also avoid the foot-in-mouth mistake we see all too often.

Create a positive epidemic

"Be the change you want to see in the world."
— Mahatma Ghandi

The start of something good.

My client in Salt Lake City started the neXus initiative by sharing it with 200 clients.

Those 200 people gave it again.

One event has become a gift to thousands and it's still growing, giving to more people each day.

Those first participants proved that giving is truly more powerful than taking, even in our modern, tech-driven business environment. They proved that the world is full of people who want to live and do business in a giving way. They proved, above all else, that one person can truly make a difference through giving.

Give your best.

About the Author

Brent Henley is a cut-the-crap consultant. He earned a masters in Industrial Psychology and went on to found The Pyramid Group in 1980, dead set on debunking the then-prevalent "smile-talk" training of the time. As you might imagine, these principles didn't always prove popular (or profitable). They did, however, build his reputation as a no-nonsense advisor who dislikes wasting time and money…and that paid off.

Today, Brent consults with the world's leading organizations from almost every sector, including Isle of Capri Casinos, Fugro, Hancock Bank, Amedisys, University of Georgia, United Way (nonprofit) and more. He's a favorite conference and convention speaker, leading insightful interactive presentations from local associations to heads of state from countries worldwide. Brent has authored and co-authored countless exercises and learning programs, many still in use by the world's leading training companies.

His plain, polite, somewhat irreverent style isn't relegated to the business world. He's an ardent fan of Jimmy Buffet, rare scotch, fine cigars and the Oklahoma Sooners (not necessarily in that order). He considers himself a father, husband and Eagle Scout (absolutely in that order).

Special Thanks

To my parents who raised me well. They gave me the freedom to be who I am while instilling great values and interest in people.

To my wife and best friend Tammy, who reminds me each day to be better than the day before.

To my family, who allows me to share so much with others.

I have to thank my good friend Jerry Lynn who continually shares his knowledge, neXus, and ideas with me and who encouraged me to write this down.

To Jeremy Broussard, one of the most creative guys on the planet, thanks for being in my neXus and doing this with me.

On my bio I list my accomplishments as Father, Husband and Eagle Scout, in that order. It says a lot, and it is my brand and who I am. I look for the same in the members of my neXus.

So can you.

More information.

To learn more about Brent Henley's consulting, availability or to inquire about a neXus workshop in your area, contact him through his organization's site, ThePyramidGroup.com.

A gift for you.

It wouldn't be right to talk about giving without giving you a few extra resources. At the book's website you'll find free, downloadable chapters on how to give through social media and the best places to meet strangers. You can also download neXus charts and other tools that make it easy to develop good "giving" habits.

That and more at ThePyramidGroup.com